SandCastle
Let's Go!

# LET'S GO
## BY
# MOTORCYCLE

ANDERS HANSON

Consulting Editor, Diane Craig, M.A./Reading Specialist

**ABDO** Publishing Company

**Published by ABDO Publishing Company, 8000 West 78th Street, Edina, MN 55439.**

Printed in the United States.

Editor: Pam Price
Curriculum Coordinator: Nancy Tuminelly
Cover and Interior Design and Production: Mighty Media
Photo Credits: Shutterstock

**Library of Congress Cataloging-in-Publication Data**

Hanson, Anders, 1980-

  Let's go by motorcycle / Anders Hanson.
    p. cm. -- (Let's go!)
  ISBN 978-1-59928-901-4
  1. Motorcycles--Juvenile literature. I. Title.

  TL440.15.H36 2008
  629.227'5--dc22

                                        2007010206

## SandCastle™ Level: Transitional

SandCastle™ books are created by a team of professional educators, reading specialists, and content developers around five essential components—phonemic awareness, phonics, vocabulary, text comprehension, and fluency—to assist young readers as they develop reading skills and increase their general knowledge. All books are written, reviewed, and leveled for guided reading, early intervention reading, and Accelerated Reader® programs for use in shared, guided, and independent reading and writing activities to support a balanced approach to literacy instruction. The SandCastle™ series has four levels that correspond to early literacy development. The levels are provided to help teachers and parents select appropriate books for young readers.

**Emerging Readers**
(no flags)

**Beginning Readers**
(1 flag)

**Transitional Readers**
(2 flags)

**Fluent Readers**
(3 flags)

SandCastle™ would like to hear from you. Please send us your comments or questions.

**sandcastle@abdopublishing.com**

**Motorcycles** are vehicles with two wheels. They carry one or two people.

3

A motorcycle has two wheels.

An engine powers a motorcycle.

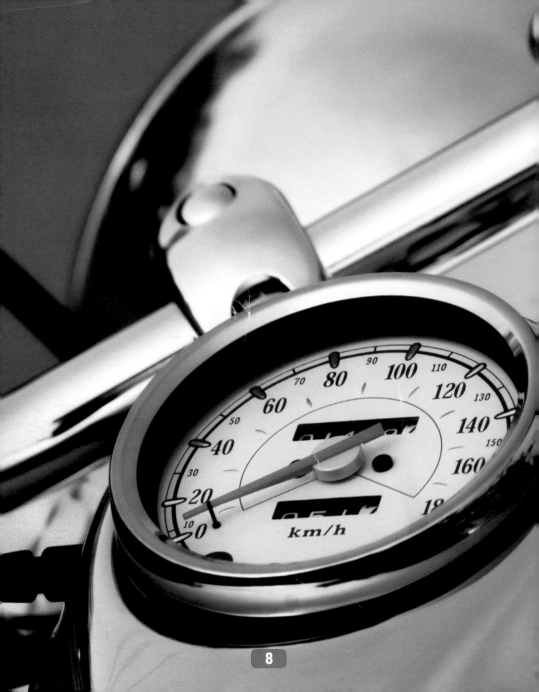

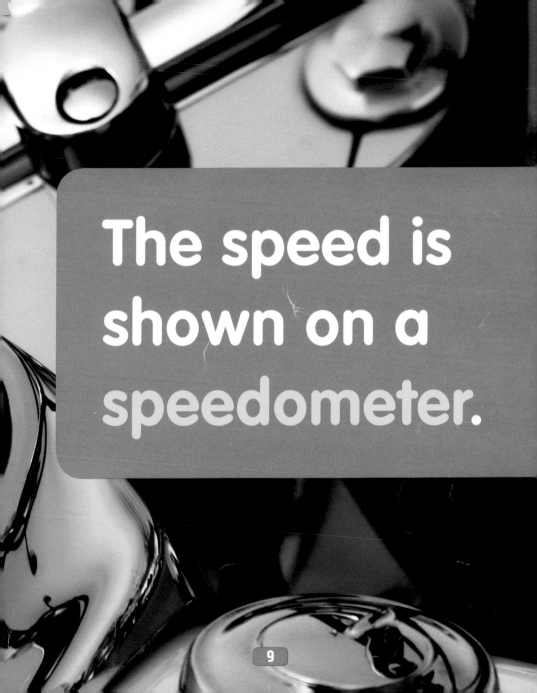

The speed is shown on a speedometer.

Engine waste comes out the exhaust pipes.

Dave can do tricks on his motorcycle.

Paul rides a tiny motorcycle called a pocket bike.

Brian and Cathy like to race their motorcycles.

James wants to
ride a motorcycle
like his father does.

# HAVE YOU BEEN
## ON A MOTORCYCLE?

# WHERE DID YOU GO?

# TYPES OF MOTORCYCLES

chopper

cruiser

dirt bike

pocket bike

scooter

sport bike

# FAST FACTS

In 1894, Hildebrand and Wolfmüller built the first motorcycle available to the public.

Every year in August, riders gather at the Sturgis Motorcycle Rally in South Dakota. In recent years, over 500,000 people have participated.

Unlike other motorcycles, most dirt bikes do not have speedometers.

# GLOSSARY

**available** – able to be had or used.

**exhaust** – the used gas and vapor released by an engine.

**participate** – to take part in.

**recent** – not very long ago.

**speed** – how fast something is going.

**vehicle** – a machine used to carry people or goods.

To see a complete list of SandCastle™ books and other nonfiction titles from ABDO Publishing Company, visit **www.abdopublishing.com**.

8000 West 78th Street, Edina, MN 55439 • 800-800-1312 • 952-831-1632 fax